SPOOKS TO SPIRITS
HISTORY & MYSTERY
HAUNTED PLACES & PLACES YOU SHOULD HAUNT
www.SpooksToSpirits.com

BY TRACEY WARD

COPYRIGHT 2010
Library of Congress Control Number 201-190-7227

Dedication

To My Wonderful Boo Crew!

My family and friends, without whom this could not have been possible.

> *Lars Ward*
> *Victoria Ward*
> *Alex Ward*
> *Kathy McCarter Welch*
> *Tara Shirriff*
> *Caitlin Halvorson*

And an apology to all my friends that I neglected to mention and love so much. Thanks for your patience.

Special thanks to:

> *The Yamhill County Historical Society*
> *Meagan and Sid Chapman*
> *Zakeri Meier*
> *MCM Channel 11*

SPOOKS TO SPIRITS
Volume 1: Lafayette-McMinnville

CONTENTS

LAFAYETTE

Chapter 1
Lafayette-The Beginning — 1

Chapter 2
Abigail Scott Duniway — 4

Chapter 3
Eva Burbank — 6

Chapter 4
Reverend Poling — 11

Chapter 5
The Curse of Lafayette — 13

Chapter 6
Pioneers to Oregon, The Peoria Party — 20

Chapter 7
The Steamboats and Locks — 25

Chapter 8
Kelty House — 28

MCMINNVILLE

Chapter 9
McMinnville   31

Chapter 10
The Cook Hotel   32

Chapter 11
The Boss Saloon   36

Chapter 12
The Hotel Oregon   39

Chapter 13
The Old Elks Building   44

Chapter 14
The McMinnville Electric Company   50

Chapter 15
Chinese Underground   51

Chapter 16
McMinnville History   56

Introduction

Spooks to Spirits is a completely new travel guide adventure to haunted places and the places you should haunt. This multimedia guide is the perfect way to get the most out of your tour. The map will keep you on track. You are already being guided by the CD. Listen carefully to stories of the destinations you are about to experience. *Spooks to Spirits* is full of mystery, history and not-to-miss dining, wine-ing and places that will stay with you a lifetime. Whether you have an afternoon or you're staying for days, *Spooks to Spirits* is informative, interesting and great for all ages - a perfect fit for the fun and the fearless.

The stories you're about to hear are true and part of our documented history, followed by present-day eyewitness accounts. Believe what you will. If you yearn for more, refer to the guide, as more unearthly stories lie within. Visit www.spookstospirits.com to find more information about the project, as well as downloadable versions of the guide, map, and CD that can be uploaded to your navigation, e-book, and music playing devices.

Spooks to Spirits will help the faint of heart find lodging, food, and that special shot of courage to face the things that go bump in the night. Take advantage of offers and savings to help you make the most of your Yamhill County Willamette Valley experience - a fun, frightening and fascinating trip. Drive carefully, stay on the road. Nighty-night and sleep tight.

Tracey Ward

My Story

In the city of McMinnville was a hundred year old home, turned into a duplex. It would be our first home. It had three bedrooms, plus a large landing up a narrow staircase that we could use as a guest room. Up the large front stair was a wrap-around balcony, and the split basement down below was such a plus. What a find! My husband and I, with our one year old son, settled in.

Moving in and setting up our home was lovely, and we looked forward to a happy time getting established in our new town. The house was an easy five block walk from downtown, and we could not wait to explore all the wonderful things McMinnville had to offer - live theatre, cool restaurants and night spots, wonderful walking and play parks, to name a few.

I first experienced something in the basement, while doing laundry. Granted, the basement was already an ominous place, dark and dank, but so what! It was about three in the afternoon. I ran down to change a load of laundry. All of a sudden the basement became very cold and even with the windows, it seemed to be getting very dark. Then I heard breathing, felt breath on my shoulder and sensed someone standing behind me. I was paralyzed, but not only with fear - I really could not move. I tried to call out and could only manage a whimper. It felt like this continued for hours. But truly, the incident lasted only fifteen excruciating minutes. Of course, my husband did not believe nor had he ever experienced anything out of the ordinary, or of the supernatural kind. He thought I just didn't want to do the laundry in the basement, and shrugged it off.

Not much happened for a few months, that WE noticed. But our son would point to the walls and say, "There it is, there it is!" Soon he would say "The face in the wall, there HE is!". Our friend's pets would go nuts and refuse to come in. We were also trying at that time the tough love bedtime - let him cry for ten minutes then check, then fifteen, and so on. Parenting itself is terrifying. Letting your baby cry when you're a mom is torture.

As we sat listening to our son cry, it changed to something else. Screaming! We ran to check. Turning on the light, we could not see him in the crib. It was like the seen from *ET*. He had managed to pull all the stuffed animals in his crib over himself. He was completely hidden in the corner, covered, screaming, "There he is! There he is!" Absolutely hysterical. It was extremely cold in his room, although it was a warm summer night. He slept with us for a while.

I had shared my concerns about these things that seemed to be getting worse, and very frightening, Still, my husband did not believe anything strange was going on. He felt there was an explanation for everything.

My husband would leave for work, sometimes at 4:30am, for the one hour commute to Portland. One morning after he was gone, I woke to find a man standing at the foot of my bed. I sat up trying to scream but nothing came. The intruder stood in front of me. I could make out his clothes and form. After a couple of minutes, this large dark figure of a man…just disappeared.

I knew what I'd seen and there was nothing friendly about it. I contacted the landlord and asked about the history of the house and inquired if anyone else had experienced problems. He hadn't had the house long and laughed me off. We started looking for a new home.

That next weekend, my husband and son were home getting ready for a play date. It was a beautiful sunny day. My son went up to get his shoes, but came down without them. He said he couldn't get them because "it is dark and scary up there." My husband told him it's a beautiful day, everything is fine, they would go upstairs together. As they went up the stairs, our normal bright landing was dark and very cold. This is the first time my husband felt that there was truly something happening. He grabbed our son, told him "Why don't we go barefoot?" and they left the house.

Our neighbors had no problems at the time. This made our experience that much harder to believe. We soon bought another home in town, built in 1894. We moved in without a problem. Our family could sleep and there was a collective sigh of relief. We started living our new life, with the living.

I don't know, but I've been told that you can buy things that can come home with spirits attached, like a blanket, a chair, or some other personal item. Perhaps. But when we moved, our neighbors started to experience knocking on their windows (ten feet up), cold spots, objects moving and a dark intruder hiding behind doors. They quickly moved. For privacy, I can't share this address with you, but I will share some more stories and the public places that you can experience yourself.

Chapter 1
Lafayette, The Beginning

Mystery and history are the foundations of this tour guide. Many of the stories outlined in this guide are well documented, though still shrouded in mystery. Other tales are fun true life accounts of the first Yamhill County settlers, including fascinating mishaps and murders involving our forefathers - frightening stories from the real people who experienced them first hand. All who have shared with *Spooks to Spirits* believe these to be true accounts.

Lafayette was officially settled by Francis Fletcher and Amos Cook in 1840. The serene valley location was fed by river traffic, surrounded by fertile fields and lush forests. An ideal place to put down roots for the early settlers. Lafayette quickly became a hub on the Yamhill River and finally the county seat. This hot spot would become the place to stop for steam ships, traders and wagon trains. By 1850 Lafayette supported 15 businesses and the county's only drug store and dentist. Yes, Lafayette, "The Glory City," was about to find itself infamous in the history and mystery of Yamhill County.

Lafayette, known as the "Athens of Oregon," seemed slated for greatness. Yet no one could imagine what would be in store for this thriving town - murder, sabotage, smallpox, bad luck, and a curse for the city to burn and fall from grace. In a hurry, you may drive through this small town without a thought. That will never happen again!

Is this the season of the witch? Folklore has it that the town of Lafayette was cursed by a woman hanged by the neck as a witch from the council tree at 2nd and Adams. There are many people who believe this to be true. On my quest to find any facts that validate these claims, I uncovered some very interesting holes in our history. These facts actually left me with a cloak of doubt, as I could not disprove this story, and here's why.

Tracey Ward

If you make your way to the corner of 2nd and Adams, your first impression is of a serene little baseball park. It took me a moment to find the rock, a monument that sits at the corner. There is a large cement flagpole a couple feet from it that dwarfs this monument. You must walk around the rock to see the plaque that reads, "At this sight, known as the Commons. The first court sessions in Yamhill County were held in 1846 under a large oak tree called the Council Oak. The first Federal Court sessions were held in 1849, Lafayette was the county seat".

Stories of people being hung in that tree abound. Here's where I ran into some problems. From 1846 to 1850 the county seat found its home in Hawks Tavern, since no court house existed at that time. In 1850, a courthouse was purchased from Lem Scott for $800. This building had been a county store and warehouse. This building burned to the ground in 1857. Arson was suspected but never confirmed. All records were destroyed except some land and probate accounts. Eleven years of history burned to ashes. We will never know if lives were lost to the council tree. This will always remain a mystery.

New courthouse built in Lafayette, 1860. Courtesy of YCHS

A new fireproof courthouse was rebuilt of bricks. Construction began in 1859 and was completed in 1860. By 1877 crime was on an upswing. A jail was commissioned and built on the northwest corner of the courthouse. It included two iron cells. I've been told the jail is still standing in Lafayette. You too, may find it, if you explore a bit! The courthouse was donated to the Evangelical Church and was used as a seminary school until 1900. After, it became a manufacturing plant for a broom factory. It was torn down in 1922.

Chapter 2
Abigail Scott Duniway

Where the courthouse once stood are a number of small businesses. The Roadhouse Pub is one and is frequented often by at least two ghosts. Full body apparitions of a woman with long dark hair and a white dress walking about the bar have been reported. Also, the spooks get touchy, tapping people on the shoulder or moving objects such as napkins on the table and paper towels from their dispensers while you visit the restroom. Both owner and manager have experienced these events. The ghost has tried to speak with the manager and wants us all to know her name is Abigail and she is not THE witch! In fact, I'm told she's a playful ghost. The Roadhouse Pub is a great stop for the ghost hunter, with wonderful clam chowder and a warm drink. But beware, this is for adults only.

Don't be disappointed little ones, Abigail has also been spotted walking the streets of Lafayette! Passers-by are often taken aback as they spot her on the side of the road, as she isn't dressed properly for the weather. Most feel concern that she may be in some sort of trouble, but she is always gone when they glance back for another look.

I did some research on the Abigail that may be still hanging around. I was lead to conclude that she might very well be the spirit of Abigail Scott Duniway. One of our most famous Lafayette citizens, Abigail became a leader in the fight for women's right to vote. She then became one of the first woman editors of the paper the *New Northwest*. A fitting title for the movement of the suffrage. Abigail also had a hand in passing the law allowing women the right to own property.

There are so many more amazing accomplishments, too many to cover. But, in her day, she would have had no problem entering places off limits to women, as a hush and lifted eyebrows of disdain would follow her across the room, her beloved husband by her side. It's no wonder Abigail still enjoys making herself known, and we know, she has a real knack for moving papers. This very exciting and interesting bit of history still lingers, reminding us that all things are possible, if we only believe.

Chapter 3
Eva Burbank

In 1853, Mr. Burbank and his wife Mary first saw Lafayette, Oregon and fell in love with all the splendor and possibilities. Despite this attraction to Lafayette, his career took precedence. Mr. Burbank would travel across the states, making a name for himself. Ultimately, he was elected to the House of Representatives.

It wasn't until 1867 that Burbank and his family would return to the place that had captured their hearts: Lafayette. Burbank became owner of a mercantile store while he continued his political involvement. The Burbank home sat on the east side of Lafayette, and Mary Burbank wrote to her friends and family that she was happy in her beautiful home, adorned with flowers, shrubbery and grounds, with a small farm adjoining.

The Burbanks had one child, Eva. She was beautiful, unusually quick and witty. Eva was a delight and charmed everyone she met. She and her mother would often take the steamboats that docked in Lafayette to Portland. They would also travel on to New York City, and abroad to Europe. She was well traveled and well spoken.

Eva had spent three years training at St. Helens Hall of Portland studying music with a focus of piano, and was touted at seventeen to be the best pianist in Oregon. For her eighteenth birthday, Eva's father commissioned a rosewood grand piano to be built for Eva. The piano, built in the East, took months to make, and would travel around the horn by clipper ship, finally arriving in Lafayette by wagon. Eva was overwhelmed to receive such a special gift. She often entertained for her family and friends, to their delight. She would play for hours, filling the Burbank home with the lush, rich tones of this rosewood piano. Eva composed and played music influenced by her travels abroad, keeping it in beautifully embellished leather books, her name embossed in gold.

Summers on the Oregon coast are spectacular. It was no surprise that Eva and a group of friends decided to holiday on the coast for a couple of weeks. The holiday started in Long Beach, and they then traveled up the coast to Astoria. It was a beautiful warm day when they reached Astoria, so the group decided to spend some time on the beach. The date was August 15th, 1880. Eva and her friends were enjoying bathing in the waves. She and a young man, Mr. Graves, were together in the surf when the unthinkable happened. They were caught in a strong undertow and carried out to sea. Eva did not know how to swim. Graves tried to keep Eva's head above water and get her to the beach, and another young man in the group raced to assist in the rescue, each trying desperately to save Eva. She and the men tired with the pounding of the waves. To everyone's horror, the group was overpowered by the breakers. The young men lost their grip on Eva, and barely made it out with their lives. Eva was lost, never to be seen again.

Although the beach was searched for months, her body was never recovered. She was 19 years, 6 months and 23 days of age. Her death threw gloom over the entire state. More than 20 pieces of poetry have been written about her sad death. Eva's memory is still cherished.

Eva's parents continued to send photos of her to the light house in hopes that she would be found, to no avail. After the death of their beloved daughter, the devastated Burbanks would even resort to trying to communicate with the dead through a spiritualist in Indiana. Perhaps she had already been communicating with them at that time. The Burbanks were consoled by the outpouring of affection that Eva received from far and wide. Charles Bray, a composer in Portland, wrote a song in her memory, "Lost in the Deep, Deep Sea." Nevertheless, the Burbanks never recovered from their loss.

The rosewood piano was donated to the Evangelical Church. The Church, built in 1892, is now the Yamhill County Historical Museum. This extremely beautiful piano, accompanied by Eva Burbank's hand-written music books, are only part of a wonderful collection of history that grace this museum, created in 1969. But more importantly, you just may experience the supernatural.

There are many reports from numbers of people that they have seen Eva playing the piano she held so dear. The museum curator's son told his mom he saw a beautiful girl playing the piano in the church. He was shocked when his mom informed him he must be mistaken, as he was the only one in the building.

A wonderful group of people volunteered when they heard the museum was in dire need of renovation. A contractor working on window panes mentioned to the curator how impressed he was at the commitment of one volunteer who went beyond the call of duty, still working long past the time everyone else had gone. The contractor actually had to sit down, when he was informed everyone had gone home long before. The church was locked and empty. Not a surprise, as Eva's most treasured piano remains on display.

Recently, a ghost hunters team came to investigate. When asked if someone wanted to let them know about their presence, the piano responded, several keys depressing all on their own. Neighbors see shadows in the windows after hours, and Eva has been seen walking through the museum straightening items. She may have been lost, but now she is found. She is still a lovely presence and a welcome addition to the mystery of Lafayette. I'm not done yet, because Eva is not alone in this church. That story is coming up.

This poem was written for Eva by her music teacher, M.P. Sadlack:

Gone in her youthful beauty,
Gone from our earth away,
Called from earth's scene of duty
On a beautiful Sabbath Day.

Fair was the flower that blossomed
Amid our band.
And prized the beauteous lily
Culled by the saviors' hand.

Sad is the home that once was.
Lit by her sweet smile's glow.
And hushed are the gentle accents,
That soothed her loved one's woe.

Yet, oh, beloved parents,
And friends most fond and dear!
Remember in your sorrow,
Thy darling is still near.

And though she's gone to heaven
To smooth your rugged way,
She, from her starry mansion,
Will watch o'er you for aye.

Chapter 4
Reverend C.C. Poling

This beautifully preserved church, now a museum, was built in 1892 under the ministry of Rev. C.C. Poling. His original pulpit is still there. Its worn edges speak to the many hours of uplifting sermons, or perhaps hellfire and damnation, that may have resonated from behind his stand.

Poling and his family resided in the rooms above. They had a happy and wonderful life in Lafayette. These were fulfilling times for this beloved family. Poling's son Daniel followed in his father's footsteps and became a world leader in church affairs, finally moving to Philadelphia to spread the Word. Poling himself also left Lafayette. But he and his son would eventually return to their home that they so loved, in the afterlife!

When visiting the museum, you may hear a child playing on the staircase. Perhaps a young father calling for his son to get dressed for church. These are the stories told by visitors who may think they are alone. They tell this to the curators, as they worry people are in an area off limits to the tour. But not to worry, Poling and his son are just keeping Eva company in this wonderful place.

If you would like to experience this marvelous museum, filled with the history and mystery of Yamhill County, just call ahead for their open hours.

Chapter 5
The Curse of Lafayette

The story you are about to hear is arguably the most famous and frightening. The Curse of Lafayette - is it a witch, or is it a gypsy?

Although many are convinced it's a witch, I believe that title would suffice for whomever experienced her wrath! Perhaps that is the answer to the confusion over witch or gypsy. There are many documented accounts of the story you are about to hear. This tale would become part of Oregon history and be included in a book titled *Necktie Parties* by Diane L. Goeres-Gardener. These necktie parties were legal executions that were carried out between 1851 and 1905.

On April 9th, 1887 at 11:00 a.m., the sharp crack of the gavel disrupted the collective gasp that resounded throughout the courthouse. The commotion did not relate to the sentence of death by hanging, but instead the last statement of the judge, "And may God have mercy on your soul." All watching felt that Richard Marple should not be give any opportunity to save his soul, because his crimes were too heinous.

Richard Marple, his wife Julia, and mother Anna, had moved to Lafayette little more than a year before. Richard, or "Gus" as he was known, was not a man who could hold down a job or do an honest day's work. He was suspected of a number of robberies that had been committed throughout the county but with no proof, no arrest could be made. Not well liked or trusted, this family, despite the rumors, maintained residence in Lafayette. His mother Anna was no better. She was smart and conniving, pulling small jobs herself. She was older, but still had her looks, and used them to beguile her unsuspecting victims.

In Lafayette, 1886, there lived a well respected and well liked 56 year old carpenter and shop keeper. His name was David Corker. He was quite successful, single and rich! This did not go unnoticed by Anna Marple, who set her sights on Corker. Anna and Corker would soon begin a lurid affair. Anna had set in motion a plan that would soon change everyone's lives forever. This plan would ultimately result in placing Anna and her son Richard in the history and mystery of Oregon, and her story, in some form or another, is still told today.

We can't know the date Anna Marple and her son Richard conceived their plan to rob her new conquest, David Corker. Richard and his mother decided that she would give Corker a sleeping powder. Richard thought himself to be knowledgeable in the use of drugs. His mother would put the sleeping drug in Corker's drink. When it took effect, Richard would enter the store through the backdoor. Simple!

All the pieces were in place and Anna had successfully given the drug to Corker. After waiting for the drug to take effect, Anna took him to the bedroom. Marple tried to enter the backdoor, but his mother had forgotten to unlock it. He then went to a side window and found it open, and entered the store. All this noise started to rouse Corker; he heard Richard come in. The drug was already wearing off.

Anna then realized that she would be the prime suspect for the robbery. At this point, Richard suggested they kill Corker and burn the building. Anna quickly found an axe and struck Corker on the forehead with a glancing blow, which only seemed to wake him. Corker was now alert! Richard grabbed the axe from his mother and started hacking away at Corker, knocking him to the bed.

Corker laid in an awkward position for left handed Richard. It was hard to get in a good blow. It took many strikes to finish the job. Blood splattered everywhere. Richard finally got in a killing blow. Gruesomely chopped about the face and head, Corker would die slowly. The Marples didn't set the building on fire, but instead arranged the body to look as if it was some kind of ritualistic killing, possibly by someone in the Masonic order. They got away with $203.

Strange noises had been heard by two teenagers passing by. The boys ran for the sheriff. Richard and his mother quickly crawled out the side window to escape. Anna and Richard didn't think about the amount of blood in the room. Richard walked through it as he left the scene.

They had planned to leave that night but decided to stay another day to throw off suspicion. A crowd gathered outside Corker's store to see what had happened. Among them was Richard Marple, joining the curious and horrified crowd as a diversion. Anna and Richard were arrested that next day. The sheriff had followed bloody footprints he had found. They lead straight to the Marple house. There he also discovered a bloody coat.

Marple explained that the blood was from a hog's head that he brought home to feed his family. Of course, he couldn't produce the hog's head and no one would believe his story.

Anna Marple was released after several weeks from the Yamhill County jail, where she and her son were being held together. They didn't have enough evidence to keep her.

Marple was cocky and denied any involvement. Instead, he tried pointing a finger at the Masons. Although that seemed far fetched, the story did cast some doubt and fear throughout the county. The Masonic order was made up of some of the most prominent men in the state. Marple would then say he was framed by the detective, whom Marple claimed took his coat to Corker's and dipped it in his blood. He would claim to be innocent to the very end.

Marple awaited his trial. The judge trying his case was Reuben Boise, a man well respected by the bar and the public for the painstaking way in which he considered each case. He would spend hours of contemplation and research in and out of the courtroom. He'd earned a reputation as a patient and meticulous judge, displaying intelligence and legal insight. In my research, I came across a story in which the judge had watched eight men die after he had passed their death sentences. But in all the other accounts I've read, I could find only two cases that resulted in death sentences. And, Marple makes three!

The day of sentencing, Marple, being found guilty, yelled at the judge saying, "You are about to sentence an innocent man and someday you will regret it!" Judge Boise pronounced the verdict:

"It is the sentence of this court that you be taken hence, and confined in the county jail until the 29th day of May, 1887 and upon said day between the hours of 10:00 a.m. and 2:00 p.m., you be taken from said jail to the place of execution and in accordance with this judgment, you be hanged by the neck until dead, and may God have mercy on your soul."

Spooks to Spirits: Lafayette-McMinnville

The crack of the gavel resounded in the courtroom. Marple was removed, as he angrily professed his innocence yet again.

The hanging day dawned bright and cold. The town was filled with spectators wanting to see this murderer hanged for his crimes. Marple had a drink of whiskey laced with opiates and refused to dress himself in the execution clothes. The sheriff had to do the disagreeable duty. Marple commented that these were the nicest clothes he had worn in ten years. Marple marched from his cell to the scaffolding, passing the waiting coffin. The death warrant was read to the crowd. Marple interrupted, "False as hell!"

The noose was placed around his neck. In the last few seconds before he was dropped, Marple turned his head and the knot in the rope slipped. Instead of a swift death from a broken neck, he was strangled slowly and painfully. Marple took eighteen minutes to die. His wife and mother watched in horror.

A blood curdling scream came from Anna Marple, who fell to her knees in despair as she watched. She then gained some composure and began to curse the people and the town of Lafayette. Her son still gasped for his last breath. She called everyone watching murderers, called for a pox upon the town. She swore that Lafayette would burn three times, and promised that Lafayette would never survive.

Anna Marple struck fear in the hearts of all who witnessed this hanging and the curse that she spat out. No one would be able to forget the events of that day. What was to follow would be met with disbelief and become part of the history and mystery of Yamhill County forever, as the curse of Lafayette continues.

You're probably wondering how I can tell you, with such detail, the story of the murder. Well, Marple's cell mate told the story, after the hanging of Marple.

Anna Marple and Julia had already moved from town, not to be found. Anna, who promised Julia half of the stolen money, would never make good on that promise. Julia and her kids disappeared from history.

Anna moved from town, but her curse remained. Lafayette would suffer. This once thriving city would soon fall, as the curse seemed to take hold.

The Yamhill River, which had been a constant source of revenue for Lafayette, started to dry up, creating mishaps for both steamboats and traders. The river would soon become too narrow to navigate. Then small pox came, killing an unknown number of residents. There was little doubt that Lafayette was losing its stronghold.

This created an opportunity for McMinnville to win the vote and capture the County seat, the year of Marple's execution. In 1890, locks were built in the Yamhill River to help continue water trade. It was too little, too late. McMinnville had already acquired the railroad, which made the water lines obsolete. Lafayette was on a downward spiral. The "Athens of Oregon" was no more. Lafayette would then burn in 1904, destroying nearly all of the city. 19 buildings, including the fire hall, were left in ashes. Lafayette was rebuilt, only to burn again in 1934.

From my calculations, either there is one more fire coming, or, let's hope Lafayette has dodged a bullet, and the fire forty years before could be counted as three. All in all, a massive exodus, and fall from power, would leave Lafayette struggling to survive.

Although Anna had moved away and died elsewhere, her spirit may have come back. Perhaps to see her curse unfold? It is believed she is still at the cemetery where her son's unmarked grave lies. Reports of a dark spirit lurking there are widespread. One man told me that, as he was sitting by the road near the cemetery, he saw a dark figure, 8 to 10 feet in height. It ran 40 yards from one tree to another. The figure wasn't solid and moved very quickly - like he did to get out of there.

Several people have told me that they have experienced blood curdling screams in the cemetery. These screams have sent the would-be ghost hunters running into the night. There are also stories of something far more sinister - a horrifying specter that actually causes physical damage by cutting intruders with razor-like fingers. I myself have yet to meet anyone who has experienced harm. But stories, fear, and the belief that something is there are plentiful.

The graveyard is a protected historic property. I can't give you an address, but it sits in a quiet area of Lafayette, unsettled to this day by a dark energy that will make itself known to anyone who dares trespass.

Chapter 6
Pioneers to Oregon, The Peoria Party

In 1812, both the United States and Great Britain lay claim to the Pacific Northwest. Since the end of the War of 1812, it was under a treaty of joint occupation. Our story begins in 1831, when a delegation of four Native Americans of the Flathead and Nez Perce tribes, who were curious about the white man's religion, set out in search of someone who could bring them the "The Book of Heaven." They went to seek the counsel of Meriwether Lewis and William Clark. Lewis and Clark had blazed the trail west, passing through the territory some twenty years earlier. Sadly, Lewis was dead, but as luck would have it, Clark was the superintendent of Indian affairs.

In St. Louis, Clark, hearing the group's interest, rallied a few churches who gathered missioners to send to Oregon in response. One who volunteered would be Reverend Jason Lee, a Methodist missionary. The group set out in 1833.

In 1838, Lee returned from Oregon with a petition for the establishment of a territorial government, signed by 36 settlers, made up mostly of Americans, 17 traders, 9 French-Canadians and 10 men that worked at the mission. The petition of 36 asked President Martin Van Buren to take possession of Oregon. This was not enough to move the president. But he agreed with Lee's idea of one thousand acres for any man over eighteen willing to make Oregon their home.

Rev. Lee decided to raise awareness of this promise by doing a number of speaking engagements. With him, he had five Native Americans from Kalapuya, part of the Chinook tribe, educated and knowledgeable. Jason Lee spoke at the Peoria Ill. Main Street Presbyterian Church. His story of generosity, plentiful food and resources sparked interest.

One of the tribesmen with Lee became ill on this visit and was left behind to recuperate. His name was Thomas Adams. Indian Tom, as he was called, created quite a sensation as he described his life in Oregon. Salmon you could reach out and catch. Corn eight feet high, beaches, timber, rain for crops, mild winters and unmatched beauty. Between Lee's speech and the stories told by Adams, it was too good to be true. But the group of young men could not help themselves. They formed a group calling themselves the "Oregon Dragoons," with the intention of claiming Oregon for the United States. There were sixteen of them in all, most in their twenties, all with high hopes but not a lot of experience. Farnham, the oldest, was made leader of the group. He wielded a flag made by his wife stating, "Oregon or the Grave," and a promise: no man left behind.

They had hopes of wealth, lots of land, and the romance of adventure. They planned to ship furs and salmon around the horn to the east, raise the United States flag and run the Hudson Bay Company out. They would rely on local trappers' maps and trader's advice en route. This would take them a month out of the way.

These men were fired up, ready to lay claim to Oregon and as unlikely as it seems, change history forever. They came to be known as "The Peoria Party." They set out the morning of May 1, 1839. Some kept diaries and their stories of this adventure are a great read! But, I'm just going to give you the highlights.

Francis Fletcher and Amos Cook were part of this party. Settling Lafayette, they remained lifelong friends and business partners. This group was terribly unprepared, running out of everything but some flour early on. They thought food would be easy to come by. But they started their trip too late in the season. As soon as bad weather set in, four of the party turned back. Hibernation and migration left the rest struggling to survive. When Fletcher brought down the first buffalo of the trip, everyone was relieved.

But though it's hard to believe, but the group's biggest problem was that they couldn't get along.

The only injury reported was due to a fight. Hot headed Sydney Smith reaching for his gun, shot himself in the side and was seriously wounded. With no doctor or medical supplies, a runner was sent to bring a doctor and borrow a wagon from a wagon train they had passed. They headed for Bents Fort, a trading post on the south fork of the Platte River.

Following the accident, the party fell into chaos and Farnham lost all authority. On the trail to Bents Fort it was slow going with the injured party. A heated meeting was held and Farnham, accused of incompetence and wasting the group's funds, was deposed as captain. Robert Shortness, who had joined the group at a Bents Fort, was elected as captain. Shortness, age 43, was eight years older than Farnham, and had lived much longer in the West. Shortness and Farnham both published accounts of their party's trip, and traded insults.

Whatever Farnham's shortcomings as a leader may have been, he saved Smith's life. Farnham cleaned and dressed Smith's wounds daily and personally drove Smith in the wagon to Bents Fort. They arrived July, 1839.

Smith then started his long road to recovery. The wagon was returned and Smith would have to ride the rest of the trip.

The party split up. Four friends, Francis Fletcher, Amos Cook, Joseph Holman, and Ralph Kilbourne, continued on. The trip from The Dalles to Fort Vancouver was the hardest part of the journey. The trails along the edge of the Columbia River were covered by high water and the men had to lead their horses by hand along the cliffs of the gorge. They arrived June 1st, 1840, 13 months after leaving Peoria, Illinois.

The four men were near starvation, with long hair and heavy beards, clad in buckskins. They traded skins for clothing. Fletcher still had some money, but was charged twenty percent to change it to British coin. This practice of the Hudson Bay Company was just another complaint that drove Americans to demand U.S. intervention in Oregon.

On the very same day the remaining 4 members of the Peoria Party made it safely to Fort Vancouver, the ship *Lausanne* arrived from New York, with Reverend Jason Lee and 40 Methodist missionaries. In company with Lee was Thomas Adams, the boy known as "Indian Tom" who had fallen ill in Peoria all those months before. Frankly, after everything these guys went through, I think I would have been a bit miffed! If they had only waited a few months, they could have taken the boat! The American colonization of Oregon was underway. Amos Cook and Francis Fletcher took adjoining land claims along the Yamhill River: the town, Lafayette.

Holman settled near Rev. Lee's church north of Salem. Ralph Kilbourne helped build the ship the *Star of Oregon* and sailed to California where he settled. Hot headed Smith was the first of the party to reach present day Oregon and became the longest living survivor of the Peoria Party. He obtained employment in the Willamette Valley from settler Ewing Young. Thomas Farnham ended up beating Robert Shortess to Oregon by two months, to Shortess's dismay. Farnham returned to the East where his journal of his western adventure was published and widely circulated in both America and Britain.

Cook, Fletcher, Holman and Smith, together with the Peoria Party veterans Shortess and Moore, voted on May 2nd, 1843 to found Oregon's first provisional government. All became influential citizens. Their biographies are recorded in the official pages of Oregon history.

You can now visit Rev. Jason Lee's home and Methodist Mission Parsonage, both built in 1841, preserved at the Mission Mills Museum in Salem.

For Cook and Fletcher, this was the start of what would be the glory days. By 1850, Lafayette became known as a "Glory City" or the "Athens of Oregon." Flatboats made water transportation on the Yamhill River a strong trading and business opportunity for the Lafayette residents. Wagon transportation during the rainy season was a serious problem; the wagons were constantly becoming stuck in the mud. Thanks to the flatboats, trade and travel could continue year-round.

Chapter 7
The Steamboats and Locks

Courtesy of YCHS

In 1851 the arrival of the *Hoosier*, a large steamboat, created a fever of excitement. The whole town of Lafayette flocked to see this beautiful ship pull into the dock. It was a much larger, faster and a more efficient craft than the flatboats, and quickly put the flatboats out of business.

This was the first of many steamboats. They became larger and more elegant, making their way to Lafayette to take advantage of a growing population of about 600. The steamboat now offered a comfortable and thrilling adventure for the early pioneers. This made for an easy trip to Oregon City or Portland. They offered good food and lodging, and were able to haul freight cheaper and faster than the flatboats.

There was so much competition at the time, the river would be overwhelmed with traffic, so much so that boats and steamboats alike could be snagged by debris and sink. Some boats were recovered, others were left behind. Some of the steamboats that braved the Yamhill early on were the *Bonita*, the *AA McCully*, the *Orient*, the *Occident*, the *Modoc*, and the *St. Church*. Along with the sunken *Elmore*, these ships shaped our history.

The steamboat *Washington*, captained by Alexander Sinclair Murray, followed the example of the *Hoosier* by also making its way up the Yamhill River on June 6th, 1851. The *Hoosier* was the *Washington's* main competition. The *Washington* ran the Yamhill County river line for several months, then decided it was too much.

After trying a number of routes, the *Washington* ended up running from Portland to Oregon City. Still the competition was fierce.

In December, 1857, downstream from Scottsburg, the career of the *Washington* and Captain Murray ended forever. A boiler explosion blew the ship apart. Captain Murray, trying to get the pressure down, was blown through the roof of his ship, landing him in a tree.

Unbelievably, Murray regained consciousness. A captain to the end, burned, battered, broken and bruised, Murray climbed down from the tree to his disabled steamboat and tried to assist the horrified crew and guests as the *Washington* sank. Though he survived, the *Washington* was a total loss. Alexander Sinclair Murray would never captain another ship, nor would he ever return to Lafayette. My hat's off to this captain, that went to such lengths to go down with his ship.

The beginning of the end. The Yamhill River started to dry up in the late 1870s. By the 1880s, no more steamships could travel to Lafayette. In 1890, to help with this problem, locks were built allowing ships to reach Lafayette once again, but it was no use. McMinnville had secured the first railroad stop for Yamhill County. A shift of power was about to take place.

The locks have been preserved at the beautiful Locks Park in Lafayette. This is a great location, whether you're stopping for the history or just a nice picnic (weather permitting).

Chapter 8
Kelty House

This colonial revival style home was built in 1872 by James Kelty and his son Paul. Some time before, James Kelty had taken Sarah Maria Scott (sister of Abigail Scott Duniway) as his wife, creating a powerful union; the elegant and serene Kelty house was their country home, enjoyed by family and friends. Sarah became quite a pianist. Perhaps she was inspired by Eva Burbank, who lived next door. Like Eva's mother, Sarah took pride in her home and the grounds, creating beautiful gardens with seating to rest and take in her creative gardening skills. The water well that sat in the gardens was equally inviting.

The proprietors of the Kelty Estate tell a story of a young child that went missing in the late 1800s. The search ended sadly as the child was found in this very deep well. Despite this tragedy, the well still remains in the garden. Only now, a wishing well has been build over the opening, in remembrance of the child and hope that happier times would come.

This would not be the case for the Kelty family, as they were about to face their own family scandal. James had became a prominent mercantile owner and sheriff, and his family was well liked and respected. Sadly, it would soon be the topic of gossip, shame and horror, brought to his doorstep via his nephew who lived in Polk county. Talk, gossip, and mystery would become a permanent part of their lives forever.

James Kelty's brother, John Kelty, was a well-to-do farmer. His son, named Oscar Kelty, was born in 1859 in Yamhill, Oregon. At the age of 25, Oscar fell in love with 18 year old Clara Glandon. He married her on September 18th, 1884 in Yamhill.

The happy couple then moved to Albany. This relationship turned sour as Oscar became abusive and violent toward Clara. Clara took her children and fled their home to seek refuge in her parents' home in Bethel, just outside the Yamhill county limits. About nine o'clock, while her father was absent, Oscar came to see Clara.

Clara came downstairs, sitting her children down on the floor and holding her 6 month old baby in her arms. Oscar asked Clara to come home with him. Clara barely had time to answer before Oscar drew his revolver and shot her. Clara fell dead onto her children, the ball passing through her and burying itself into the piano.

Oscar escaped, but was soon arrested as he tried committing suicide. Everyone was so overwhelmed by his cowardly and murderous deed that a lynch mob formed. On July 7th, 1887, Oscar was taken out and hanged until he was dead.

The grieving family members, cut so deeply by the shock and horror of these events, never recovered.

This story recently came to life when the great grandson of Oscar began to research his family history. He discovered that when Oscar shot his wife, it was his grandfather she held in her arms. The child suffered severe powder burns that disfigured his face. He told his grandchildren that he had a bad skin condition, and kept the family secret until he died. What a burden for a boy to bear for his entire life.

The Kelty house was converted into a bed and breakfast, and new visitors are always welcome. If you make the Kelty house your stay, sleep well, although there are other unexplained visitors that may join you.

There are reports of a gentleman standing at the top of the stairs or in the hallway, in full dress top coat and a tall top hat. Perhaps he is dressed for an evening out with his beloved wife. The front hall goes cold even in summer. Unexplained footsteps, and the voice of a child talking in the other room, have been heard.

All reports say these other visitors are kind and interesting. I'm guessing they're still trying to find their way home, or just coming to a warm familiar place. You can experience this wonderful place too, and wake up to the smell of an amazing breakfast hand-prepared by the proprietors. Who knows what you may uncover.

Chapter 9
McMinnville

My first visit to Oregon was under a dusting of ash. Mount St. Helens had just erupted and the sky was filled with ash that looked like snow. It was later that same year, in 1980, when I settled in McMinnville. Falling in love with the beauty and seasons that are Oregon and finally experiencing real snow was truly magical.

McMinnville is in the heart of Yamhill County, Willamette Valley, Oregon. It is surrounded by hundreds of wineries and fascinating small towns rich in history, mystery, lush views and artistic people.

Driving through downtown McMinnville in the spring, the streets are lined with flower baskets. The charm and beauty of the area is overwhelming. The architecture will draw you in as our heritage unfolds before you.

In the winter the trees that line both sides of the street are lit with twinkling lights. Although our winters are wet, I believe it adds to the ambience of the town. Wet streets glisten with long lines of color that stream from all the warm and inviting establishments of downtown McMinnville. Your trip will stay with you for a lifetime - the people, the surrounding countryside, or perhaps something else entirely.

Tracey Ward

Chapter 10
Cook Hotel

On the 500 block of downtown McMinnville you won't be able to miss the very cool theater called the MACK, a beautifully done example of turn of the century architecture and Art Deco style renovation. This building was constructed in 1887. At the time it was called the Cook Hotel, a three story masonry with Italianate and Queen Anne detailing. It was named for the proprietor, Lyman Hall Cook, who was joined by his wife Lydia Jane Reed and their two children. The Cook Hotel was a welcome addition to the growing town.

As a hotel, the Cook would house many prominent officials, as well as working men and families looking for a restful nights sleep or perhaps waiting for their own homes to be built. The Cook sported 28 rooms, a fancy parlor, luxurious bridal chamber, billiard parlor and dining room. It has been rumored there was a balcony that wrapped around two sides of the building. The Cook served as a wonderful refuge for the weary traveler for many years.

As the years went on the Cook Hotel faced competition from another hotel built to meet the needs of the growing population. On the 700 block was The Douglas Hotel, not as fancy and more affordable. Cook passed away in 1890, just three years after the opening of his hotel. The Cook Hotel was then renamed the Hotel Yamhill.

In 1905 Hotel Elberton (now known as Hotel Oregon McMenamins) had opened kitty corner from the Hotel Yamhill. The face of McMinnville was changing. The Hotel Yamhill was forced to change its vision as well. At this point, the idea of using the street level as storefronts became a reality.

By 1930 the renovation of the hotel was complete, turning it into the Art Deco theater you see today. The building still serves as a storefront to Serendipity Ice Cream and the wonderful Thistle restaurant. The casualty of the renovation was the closure of the two floors upstairs, and we await the reopening of the MACK theater itself.

As sad as this sounds, the Hotel Yamhill stills remains a busy place to stay - at least for the spirits that linger! There are numerous stories of hauntings in the hotel. I've been told by a few people about cold spots in the bathroom, and the feeling of being watched when they were alone closing the theater. The ghost hunting company of C.A.S.P.E.R. even did an overnight investigation in 2007.

I was able to connect with three of the party involved in that experiment. What follows is a recap of what they shared. The stories may be a bit different from what you may have seen on their show, because for that they all need to collaborate or they would not share the information. I got the real skinny on what these members saw and heard - and also learned that some of the party got so scared they had to leave the project.

In the theater an EVP (electronic voice phenomenon) was recorded in answer to the question, "Is someone here? Try to speak?" They caught the reply of an old man in a very deep voice: "I never did that before."

When filming in the lobby, a vague image of a woman standing by the doorway was caught in the mirror. Later someone called out the name "Katie."

Then the crew went to Serendipity Ice Cream. In the night, in the quiet, the investigators started asking questions. This time an answer came in the form of a light bulb exploding above the counter. That was unnerving, but it was the full body apparitions of a young woman with her child that were really off-putting. They were dressed in white, she in little black boots. They held hands as they descended the closed-off staircase.

The group split up as one of the members went to the restaurant next door, where the Thistle now resides. Loud noises came from the basement, as though something heavy had dropped. As the team headed down the stairs, checking for possible reasons, they heard footsteps. Those footsteps started up the stairs. They were heavy, loud, and no one was there.

At this point the group headed upstairs to the hotel. There they experienced equipment failure as footsteps again headed towards them. Finally, a few decided this was enough. They left the hotel. The crew who stayed recorded more EVPs of a number of different scenarios, as you would hear if you were in a bustling hotel. Multiple conversations were heard, in different areas of the building, all at the same time. Two women talking in one room, men in another. On the second and third floors, more people talking. Now a clear conversation between man and wife:

"Hey Lisa?"

"I'm busy!"

This was followed by something chilling at the other end of the hotel - a man's voice, quiet at first, then louder and louder until it echoed through the hallways: "Help...*Help*...HELP!"

In a back room stood a tall man in a cowboy hat and boots. The man disappeared, but the footsteps from the boots walked right toward the group. The investigation was over.

I did some research and came across the story of Samuel W. Gardner, a 72 year old cowboy and farmer at the end of the 19th century. Grieving after the death of his wife five months prior, Samuel checked himself into the hotel. He stayed there until he died from heart failure and pneumonia at 12:50pm, 1891. He had been sick for a week, said a report, but perhaps he was just waiting to meet his wife in a place that had meaning for them. Maybe Samuel is the tall man in the cowboy hat?

There is no doubt that people are still staying at the Hotel Yamhill. Some for fun! Others possibly with unfinished business. Stop in for an ice cream or treat yourselves to a wonderful meal and see if you make any new friends.

Chapter 11
Boss Saloon (La Rambla)

In 1884 an unknown person built the first brick building on Third Street in McMinnville. In 1905 this building, now titled the Schilling building, was stuccoed and the beautiful crown and detailed cornice work was added. The builder had some insight. The town's main road at that time was Baker Street, aka Highway 99, named after the town's first settler. But it turned out that the amount of travel by wagons, bad weather, and soft soil made Baker Street a mess. The main street would soon be relocated to the Third Street you see today. This change brought many thirsty travelers to the Boss Saloon, the first bar built inside the Schilling building.

The Boss Saloon was a welcome watering hole for the weary traveler and the working men in the area. Many glasses were raised in toast and tipped in promise and in sorrow. It housed many looking for a place to rest weary feet, or find a fight and burn off pent-up anxiety. It also became a welcome stopover for the men of the wagon trains, on their way to an unknown future. The Boss Saloon was a bar with many stories of trials, tribulations and the pride that came with the creation of a new town.

Within the next ten years the growth of McMinnville would exceed all expectations. The Yamhill County Bank building, built in 1888 on the corner of Third and Cowls, dwarfed the Boss. Soon the saloon would be no more, as many other saloons cropped up to replace it.

The Boss went through many transformations, and became a grocery store, a five and dime, and a bed factory, to name a few. It even would house a head shop, while the owner at the time, Mr. Rutherford, resided upstairs. Sadly, the building went through some tough times and fell into disrepair, finally staying empty for years.

In 2002 Kathy Stoler purchased the building. With amazing vision, she successfully completed one of the most extensive and beautiful renovations in our town, saving this treasure. La Rambla at 238 NE Third Street is now one of our most prized locations. With the surrounding elegance and inspired cuisine from Spain, it's a must see. But wait, you know I wouldn't be telling you this story if there wasn't the chance you might meet some new friends.

Tracey Ward

The guests that grace this establishment should keep a watchful eye. There is a bit of humor, as well as bothersome spirits, hanging around. The bartenders and wait staff can tell you stories of moving chairs, spigots opening and pouring drinks onto the floor while they watch, and things flying from one side of the room to the other. Lights will flicker as you hear the switch being turned on and off. Sweet smells of perfume will resonate in cold spots on warm nights.

My husband and I know a couple who went out for a well deserved drink and hors d' oeuvres. On a dark and rainy night, they made their way to La Rambla and waited at the end of the bar until a table opened. She hung her coat on the back of her chair and her husband placed his feet on her chair rail as they leaned in to visit. The scene was set for a romantic evening.

Someone behind her hit her with the back of their chair. She thought with the coats, rain, etc., it was an accident, no problem. Her husband, meanwhile, was off his barstool. He was convinced the floor has a slant, moving his barstool away from hers. Again she was hit in the back. Now she's getting a bit miffed, but shrugged it off. She watched her husband checking the bottom of his barstool because he had slid away again. The third time she was hit in the back, she turned to say, "Excuse me!!" No one was at the bar! They paid their tab and as they walked out, her husband said, "Something strange happened to me in there!" He felt he was being pulled away from her on his barstool when it happened a third time! She replied, "Me too!" and told him about the unexplained hits.

I'm guessing someone didn't like them together. All in all, it made for a fascinating and memorable outing. They keep returning to La Rambla, and so far have not had any more unexplained interactions.

Experiencing a haunting doesn't mean you see apparitions. There doesn't need to be big grand gestures. Most experiences are small and understated, and many times will go unnoticed. La Rambla is a not-to-miss spot, with a great menu and the possibility of meeting some interesting guests - if you pay attention.

Chapter 12
Hotel Oregon

Originally the Hotel Elberton, built in 1905, was only two stories and cost $15,000 to complete. Thomas A. White, a restaurateur and farmer, stood proudly as the proprietor when the hotel's doors opened. With beauty and great service, the hotel became popular right away. It attracted businessmen and transit workers. Students and professors would also stay as Linfield College (then McMinnville College) gained in notoriety.

The builders, Fenton and Link, were hired to add two more floors in 1910, but were only able to complete the third floor. The fourth floor would remain unfinished for nearly 80 years - the perfect formula for the unseen guests who just didn't want to leave. As with most of the buildings downtown, there were ups and down for this hotel. In 1932 the first story was renovated, adding the elevator, quite a luxury. The hotel's named was then changed to Hotel Oregon. But still the lull in business made it necessary to offer the street front to businesses to help with revenue. A barber shop and a real estate office were the first to move in.

In 1946, (during WWII) a Portland Hotel owner Arnold "Nic" Nicolai and his brother bought the hotel. The brother entrepreneurs opened the Paragon Room restaurant and lounge. The true original Naugahyde and wood paneled room gained notoriety as a great steak house. The brothers also brought in popular music and musicians of the day, making the hotel a destination spot once again.

But all the king's horses and all the king's men could not keep the rain from coming in. 1950 to 1970 again saw a rotation of businesses to help the hotel survive. The Paragon Room closed it doors in 1958. The hotel now hosted a number of companies over the years, including the Greyhound bus depot, a snack shop and taxi stand.

The hotel's fate went from bad to worse. A water pipe burst during a freeze in 1967, damaging many of the rooms and making them uninhabitable. Costs prohibited repair. The bus depot was replaced by the Beauty Maid Shop that stayed there for forty years. There was also Grandma's Wedding Shop, which started as Grandma's Doll House but was changed when her fancy turned to love; this wedding shop remained for over 10 years. The Cat's Meow found a home where the hotel lobby once was. The staircase and elevator were walled up. The three floors of this once magnificent hotel became a distant memory - but this left even more space for lost souls, filled with the memories of the glory days, to roam.

Grandma's Weddings still exists today on Highway 99W. The original owner, Juanita, is there sewing her sequins and pearls to her beautiful gowns, and will share her stories with you of her stay in the Hotel Oregon. I will share a few, as well some others I've gathered from employees and guests.

Juanita would sit in her back room working. She'd be happy to hear her door bell jingle, letting her know she had a costumer - then surprised to find no one there. This would happen again and again. After 8 or more times, Juanita felt the presence "of a mischievous child," and named him John. She would tell him, "John, knock it off," and he would.

There were many other incidents. Her bathroom down the dark hall would open and close on its own. She finally tied it open. Still Juanita could hear the creaking of the door opening and closing, and when she checked, it would still be tied to the wall. She hung all her veils from the ceiling, putting them there by ladder. As she sat in her rocker, a veil would slowly fall, as if floating to the floor. She would comment, "So you like that one do you?" Candles from the candelabras on the buffet would be lined up on the floor in the morning, or things would be left in the middle of the room.

 The one thing Juanita would never do was be there at night.

The Cat's Meow was also a shop in the hotel. An employee shared with me years ago their frustration at having to put back into place the pictures and items that decorated the blocked-off staircase. It seems they had many poltergeist problems. This was so interesting to me, as when visiting with the McMenamin's historian, he told me Hotel Oregon is their only property with poltergeist activity!

The McMenamins brothers, well known for their restoration of historic locations, were a welcome sight. They came to McMinnville in 1990 and fell in love with the idea of bringing the Hotel Oregon back to life - a huge undertaking. Each room and every floor, including the fourth, was painstakingly brought back to its original glory. Then even more was added - the history of all the people that helped make this hotel and our county the wonderful place it is today. Artwork covers the walls with the history of those past, and possibly still present!

There are areas that seem to have constant activity. The third floor housekeepers get frustrated at the beds being unmade right after they have made them. They will place glasses on shelves and find them moved to different locations when their backs are turned. Perhaps some lingering staff have their own way of doing things.

A group of four women checking out each other's rooms found a man standing in the window. Not to worry, as he disappeared before they could excuse themselves for being in the wrong room.

The elevator has a mind of it own. and if you listen closely you may hear what was once picked up on an EVP: a woman saying, "Makes its own stops!" Walking the hallways you may hear or feel other guests walking behind or in front of you. Well, at least they were guests at one time.

The fun and well trained bartenders in the rooftop bar have a little girl who wants to talk to them. While they are in the storage closet they will hear a sweet little "Hello!" Many have spent time looking for her, as it is a bar - no place for a little girl - but to no avail, only to be met with that little

"Hello!" while stocking and setting up or breaking down for the day.

The cellar bar also has a number of visitors, not all of them visible. Items move on shelves to different places, sometimes falling. One gentleman, named Fred by employees, loves to smoke his cigar. The fragrant scent fills the room. Of course no smoking is allowed, but this is a little hard to enforce with Fred. You may hear laughing, or maybe someone whispering, "I can see you!"

Playful and warm memories of the glory days - how nice they still have this wonderful place to stay. You can stay there too! A walk into our past.

Chapter 13
The Old Elks Building

On the 500 block of 3rd Street is a beautifully restored building that dates back to 1908: the Old Elks Building. It has many storefronts, including high end boutiques, unique shopping and two restaurants. The second story is a 9000 sqare foot apartment that incudes a ballroom. The owners of this historic gem are the second owners of this building.

Originally the second floor was the Elk's club, but they moved out in 1936 and for most of the time since the upper floor was vacant. In the '60s the ballroom was used as a teen center. It is currently under renovation and still has some paintings of hip cartoon characters gracing the walls from its teen center days.

The ground floor originally had the first formal movie theater in McMinnville, with seats graduating down - very classy. Among the memorabilia, photos and posters found in the attic the owners also found the pieces of the original theater ticket booth, which they reconstructed.

The shops saw many changes over the years. In 1930 one of them became the Pair-A-Dice Tavern. I know many locals still remember that bar, and mementos of its past still remain - such as the bullet hole in a light fixture, left after an angry brawl resulted in a gunfight.

The owner's restoration is still ongoing but the finished areas are breathtaking and done to perfection. The massive dinning hall, seating rooms with fireplaces, bedrooms, and a perfectly appointed kitchen are restored to their original Arts and Crafts period. This is truly a beautiful home!

It's a good thing they have all that room, because they also have quite a few visitors.

On a couple of occasions the owner has followed a woman he thought was his wife, calling out her name only to find that she was in an entirely different part of their home. At first extensive checks were done of the house, thinking someone had broken in. There was no evidence of a break in, and the woman was never found. The second time he followed a woman through the house another search took place. Again, no intruder was discovered.

While getting ready to host a large event, a trusted friend was helping to set up. She was approached by who she thought was a maid saying, "Don't mess up the floors!" They have no maid.

Tracey Ward

While workers did some renovation, the owner decided to use the office in the attic, a quiet place in the storm of work happening around him. He was a bit put off when he heard loud knocking on the wall. It continued to grow more annoying and so loud he was having trouble thinking. He went to see what the workers were doing.

Nothing was going on where the noise was coming from and the workers said they hadn't been working in that area. But after returning to the attic, the knocking continued. The owner walked toward the sound. There were some doors laying against the wall and he realized the knocking was coming from one of them, a door that went to nowhere. He no longer goes to the attic.

Their daughter and her husband even refuse to spend the night. The deciding moment happened when one night the son-in-law woke to his blankets being pulled back. That was it.

The family has taken some pictures around the house. Once developed, they discovered something unusual. There where frames of orbs floating through the ballroom. In other pictures of the same room, sometimes taken within seconds of the others, there was nothing. Take a look at the photos at the end of the chapter to see what I mean.

One carpenter who has worked in the building for years has started talking to the residents while he works. He tries to let anyone there know that his intentions are good and he's only trying to improve their home.

This amazing home is just the crown on the head of amazing shopping and dining. Be sure you stop in and do explore, as each storefront comes with their own stories and secrets. A great way to cap off a day of wine tasting, or just to meet and greet our locals and soak up some local color.

Tracey Ward

This photo was taken at 8:53pm on March 20, 2011.

Spooks to Spirits: Lafayette-McMinnville

This was taken at the same location, the same day, just two minutes later.

Tracey Ward

Chapter 14
The McMinnville Electric Company

This historic building houses some of the finest spirits (wine) in the county. The tasting room is opened 12 to 5 most days. But the real activity starts when the doors close. Reports of activity from workers have been rampant for years. Some past employees shared with me they refused to be there alone after dark and would invite a friend along. That friend also experienced the spirits - not the wine - and refused to tag along ever again.

The side door handle will turn 360° back and forth - of course no one is there. In the kitchen and tasting room lively conversations are had between unseen men, and footsteps are heard in the bathroom area and in the attic. The full body apparition of an older man has been seen walking through the wine barrels, probably checking on the current vintage and making sure everything is as it should be. I think he's finishing up so he'll be ready for the jam - music that is! Yes, reports of music, the back porch kind of blues, have been reported. A beautiful place to enjoy wonderful wine, and in time maybe you too will get an invite to the spirit filled party! Keep your eyes and ears open.

Chapter 15
Chinese Underground

Under the streets of McMinnville is a well kept secret. In Seattle, Portland, and Pendleton you can take tours of an underground world of catacombs and lost cities. There are no such tours here, and few people even know that an underground world exists, but under the McMinnville streets lay the dark and unmistakably mysterious remnants - a Chinese city! Tunnels, opium dens, restaurants, sleeping quarters, laundry, shoe repair, blacksmith, chicken coops, a tavern and gambling rooms, all very organized and very spooky. Chinese words on a board at the entrance gave me pause, as I was able to see this world for myself. The well preserved and surprising history lies dormant beneath our feet.

Chinese immigrants took the long trip across the ocean at a cost of 50 dollars, a debt to be repaid. In the 1860s the Chinese were making the trip from China to California for the same reasons everyone was coming to the west coast - to make their fortune in a new world. The "Coolies," as they were called, did many dangerous jobs and were essential in the building of the railroad. They were expert craftsman at stone work, trestles and tunneling through the mountains. They created strong massive works and were meticulous and industrious laborers.

But even in the free world they would become owned or indebted to their boss - not just their employer, but a Tong. The Tong would be like a gang leader in today's world. The Tong would negotiate the terms and payments the worker would receive. The promise to travel to the new world, with a chance of earning $800 to $1000 to take home to their families, motivated most of these immigrants. The rate of pay could be a dollar a day. But the Chinese workers were encouraged by their Tong to gamble and smoke opium, spending their money, so the chance of returning home became more and more unlikely.

They were also forced, under threat of beheading, to wear Manchu costume dressing. This included shaving the front of their heads and combing the rest of their hair into a "Queue," a long ponytail. This was an expression of loyalty to the Manchu Qing Emperor. A Chinese male who had cut his Queue, by Manchu law, could not return to China.

The long ponytail that hung from their hats resulted in the slang name "Coolie," which helped incite discrimination and hatred. In 1870 there was an economic crisis. Many Americans lost theirs jobs. This was the start of an "anti-Chinese" movement. The focus on the Chinese workers became stronger and attacks, riots, racist violence and massacres spread throughout the West.

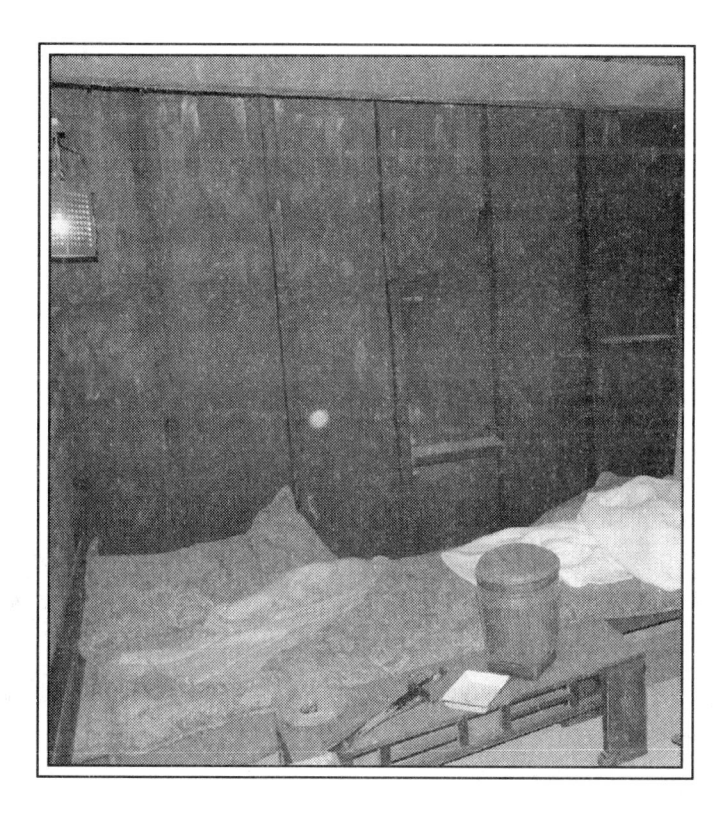

In 1882 the Chinese Exclusion Act was passed. The Chinese were no longer able to enter the country. The men now were forced into less favorable jobs. It was dangerous to be seen after dark. Many fled to California and other large cities that may afford them the opportunity to make a living.

In McMinnville there is no evidence of Chinese women living in town. Male workers were allowed as they were good for field work, farming and building. The men that stayed ultimately moved underground. It seemed that most building owners didn't care about the happenings beneath them, allowing a underground habitat to be engineered. It became more than just a habitat, it became a city! Tunnels ran from business to business underground. This afforded the Chinese a way to do their jobs, laundry, cleaning, and construction, all without being seen.

Still, on occasion a drunken cowboy would catch a Chinese worker and cut off his Queue for fun. Then the abused man was not just dealing with discrimination above ground - he must also face his Tong. These men could face death at their own people's hands. The reports I've read claim that there was much violence among the Chinese. There was no empathy for a man who was ill, wounded or had lost his expression of loyalty to the Manchu Qing Emperor. Danger was inside and out.

The census of 1890 claimed 10,000 Chinese lived in Oregon. By 1920, only 2000 remained.

I came across a story that a Chinatown in Corvallis was burned to the ground in the twenties by the Ku Klux Klan. I understand Salem also has found a Chinese underground. Perhaps these too will be open to the public in the future.

In Pendleton, the underground city was discovered when the streets started sagging. An amazing look into our past was unearthed and still remains an eerie reminder of the early beginnings of the city, with stories and questions still left unanswered.

The only underground you can experience in McMinnville today is the Cellar Bar under The Hotel Oregon. Pay attention to the skylights that sit on the sidewalk above. These skylights are the main light source for the underground. The back door to the alley would be a silent escape to the world above. There are many stairways to nowhere around town; as you stroll the streets of McMinnville you may find other tell-tale signs underfoot of our past. But any place you may visit in McMinnville will lend you the chance of meeting a quiet stranger, if only caught by the corner of your eye, as they still prefer to remain unseen.

Spooks to Spirits: Lafayette-McMinnville

Tracey Ward

Chapter 16
McMinnville History

McMinnville got a late start with just a few settlers. In 1844 John G. Baker made his way across a peaceful stream to find a lovely pasture surrounded by trees. He knew at once he had found the spot he would call home. He built his home, a 14 by 16 foot log cabin without a floor, windows, or doors. Only a blanket covered the entrance. The soil was rich and he was sure that his crops would be good. He then brought his wife and two young sons who had been waiting at Fort Vancouver and took advantage of his squatter's rights on 640 acres.

Curious Indians pulled back the blanket of their home more than a few times to see the white woman and the children. A bit nerve-racking, but no harm ever came to this family at the hands of the Indians. Still, I think I would have had my husband build me a door and some shutters!

The name *Yamhill* was derived from the local Indian name of "yamel," meaning "a ford" - a shallow crossing on the river. A tribe of Kallapuya Indians lived in the area; they were a peaceful and quiet group of Indians. Sadly, by 1910 smallpox and other misfortunes had wiped out all but five of the tribe.

Following closely in Baker's footsteps was William Newby. Newby and Baker had been in the same party coming west in 1843, called "The Great Migration." The two became good friends, and Newby took the parcel next to Baker.

Samuel Cozine also came to McMinnville and settled south of Newby. He was said to have a "buoyant spirit," happy and personable. In 1845 he had saved enough money to propose to his love. He had fallen in love with a girl he had courted on the trip across the plains. He then purchased Thomas Owen's Donation Land Claim and built a small cabin. The claim was also for 640 acres, which seemed to be the going lot size at the time. Samuel built a small blacksmith shop and served the farmers in the area.

There are reports of both Newby and Cozine donating land to the college and church. You can visit Samuel Cozine's home. It stills sits on the corner of Baker and Third and houses the McMinnville Downtown Association. Samuel's whimsical home is a fine example of his light sense of humor and the love he brought to everything he did.

Newby built the first grist mill in 1853 below the present day library at the end of Third Street. It was a blessing to the farmers who no longer had to haul their crops to Oregon City. It became the largest business in the area and was a hub of activity. This one endeavor would be the start of something big. Newby soon asked his friend Cozine to move his blacksmith shop to adjoin the mill. In 1854 a traveling peddler Solomon Beary hung up his walking shoes to open a general store on Newby's land by the mill.

Newby realized that to create a truly strong city, there must be a close-knit area of homes and businesses. To encourage this, he allowed some families the right to build their homes on his land on four acre parcels, and also maintained that these gifts of land become legal so the owners would be in title of their property. He then donated five acres as the town site. Newby set forth the groundwork and watched the town come alive before his eyes.

William Newby was a man who truly had a vision of the powerful city and gave of himself, his land and his money to make that happen. Ultimately the city of McMinnville was named after Newby's hometown of McMinnville, Tennessee.

Saboteur or entrepreneur? Our beloved founding father is a hero here in Yamhill County. But some people in Lafayette don't hold him in such regard.

The story of the loss of the Yamhill County Seat to McMinnville is one cloaked in folklore and suspicion. Some stories tell of a wild group of gunslinging thieves on horseback that broke into the courthouse and stole the records in a cloak of darkness. Well, maybe theft is a strong word, but the truth of how McMinnville won the county seat from Lafayette is equally disturbing.

Newby's vision was large. He knew the only way to win the county seat would be to win the railroad. He approached the newly founded Willamette Valley Railraod Company and found Mr. Joe Gaston. Gaston already had plans drawn for the railroad to go down the Willamette River to California. Lafayette was to be a major stop. Newby suggested the railroad bypass Lafayette and instead come to McMinnville. Gaston let Newby know that it wasn't financially possible, as they would have to build two bridges over the river instead of the one to Lafayette. However, Gaston was swayed when Newby offered $100,000 for materials and labor. McMinnville won the route.

The time had come for the vote. Lafayette and McMinnville were equally matched in population at that the time, but when the vote was tallied McMinnville had won. Folklore has it that the train was sent out of the county to retrieve people to weigh the vote in McMinnville's favor; some even said a dinner was promised. Of course, I haven't found any record of that (as if I would). What's interesting to me is that the plans for the court house and groundbreaking for the building was already underway. Someone was pretty confident.

Conclusion

Enjoy your stay!

The history and mystery of this wonderful place is palpable. I can't possibly tell you all the stories I uncovered in Lafayette and McMinnville, as I need to move to the next city. You will have to take advantage of the hints and clues given, so you can unearth your own moments and memories of the history and mystery awaiting you in Yamhill County Oregon.

Make your trip to Yamhill County a wonderful and memorable one. Look around you and enjoy the rich history that laces these streets, above and below. Pay attention to the things that may cross the corner of your eye, odd smells, cold spaces and the things that go bump in the night. Reminisce of what was.

Spooks to Spirits gives you all the tools and information you may need. Follow the guide to haunted places and the places you should haunt! Each unique building has its own story. Make your trip your own. Stop and enjoy, ask and investigate. At the very least, you will be enchanted and moved by every moment of your stay.

If you think this might be the place for you, don't be surprised when you sign that lease, as some come with a paranormal clause! And remember, if you happen to get a tap on the shoulder and no one is there, just say "Hello!"

Spooks to Spirits Travel Guide
Let local businesses serve all your needs!

Fine Dining
Bistro Maison
Fresh Palate Café
The Joel Palmer House
Kame Restaurant
La Rambla Restaurant
Legends Restaurant - Spirit Mtn. Casino
Nick's Italian Café & Back Door
Olive You

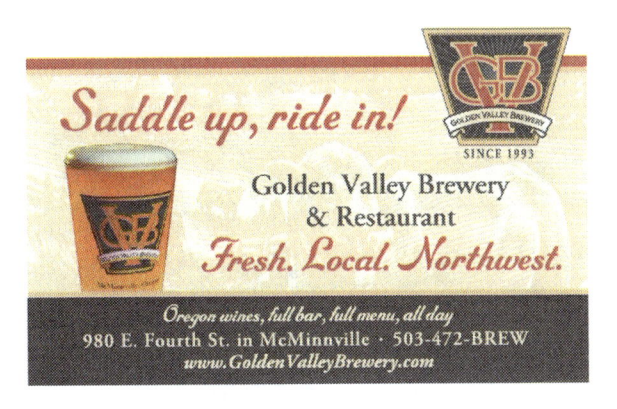

Saddle up, ride in!

Golden Valley Brewery & Restaurant
Fresh. Local. Northwest.

Oregon wines, full bar, full menu, all day
980 E. Fourth St. in McMinnville · 503-472-BREW
www.GoldenValleyBrewery.com

Cielo Blu

fine Italian food
119 W Main St. Carlton, OR
503-852-6200
cieloblurestaurant.com

One of the nation's most wine friendly restaurants!
Wine Spectator & Wine Enthusiast

Open Daily
FOR LUNCH & DINNER

WEEKDAYS
HAPPY HOUR
4 TO 6 PM

LA RAMBLA
NW Inspired Cuisine from Spain
238 NE THIRD STREET
MCMINNVILLE · 503.435.2126
laramblaonthird.com

If you would like to advertise with Spooks To Spirits, visit our website:
www.spookstospirits.com

Spooks to Spirits Travel Guide
Let local businesses serve all your needs!

Casual Dining
Cedar Plank Buffet at Spirit Mountain Casino
Haagenson's Catering & BBQ/Ribslayer to Go
American Legion Veterans Club
Dragon Gate Restaurant
Golden Valley Brewery & Pub
Harvest Fresh Grocery & Deli
Jake's Deli Restaurant
McMenamins - Hotel Oregon
Third Street Pizza Company
Yan's Chinese Restaurant
Sage Café

Bed & Breakfast
Baker Street Bed & Breakfast
Brookside Inn On Abbey Road, LLC
Lobenhause Bed & Breakfast
RR Thompson House B&B
Wine Country Farm
Youngberg Hill Vineyards & Inn

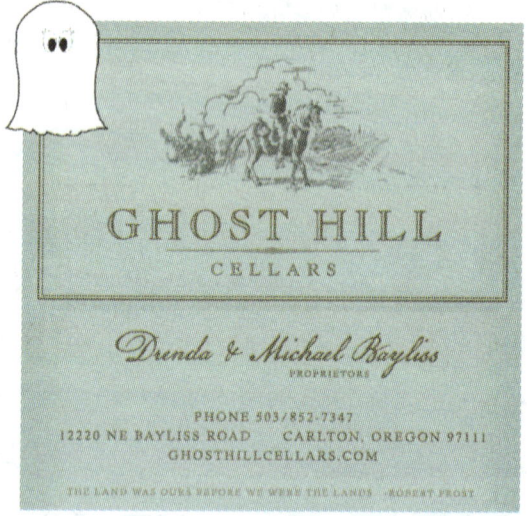

GHOST HILL CELLARS

Drenda & Michael Bayliss
PROPRIETORS

PHONE 503/852-7347
12220 NE BAYLISS ROAD   CARLTON, OREGON 97111
GHOSTHILLCELLARS.COM

THE LAND WAS OURS BEFORE WE WERE THE LANDS -ROBERT FROST

Harvest Fresh Grocery & Deli
251 NE Third Street • McMinnville
(503) 472-5740 HarvestFresh.com

If you would like to advertise with Spooks To Spirits, visit our website:
www.spookstospirits.com

Spooks to Spirits Travel Guide
Let local businesses serve all your needs!

Motels
Best Western Vineyard Inn Motel
Comfort Inn & Suites
Inn at Red Hills
McMenamins - Hotel Oregon
Red Lion Inn & Suites
Spirit Mountain Lodge

Vacation Rentals
A Tuscan Annex
LePetite Chateau
Oregon Wine Cottage
Red Ridge Farms
The Pinot Quarters
Wine Country Cottage

Banquet Facilities
Evergreen Aviation Museum
Golden Valley Brewery
Jake's Deli & Restaurant
Michelbook Country Club

Coffee Shops
The Coffee Cottage
Cornerstone Coffee Roasters
Coyote Joe's Coffee Co.
Dutch Bros.
K&F at Union Block
Starbucks

Catering
Bon Appetitte
The Fresh Palate Café
Wine Country Catering
Jake's Deli & Restaurant
Harvest Fresh Grocery & Deli

Antonio's Italian Restaurant
Dine In or Take Out
Open for Lunch & Dinner
(503) 864-4182
416 E. 3rd St.
Lafayette, OR 97127
Monday thru Friday 11:30 AM - 9 PM
Saturday & Sunday 1 PM to 9 PM

At our historic hotels, you never know what – or who – you'll find around the corner...
HOTEL OREGON McMinnville · (503) 472-8427
GRAND LODGE Forest Grove · (503) 992-9533
McMENAMINS HISTORIC HOTELS
mcmenamins.com

If you would like to advertise with Spooks To Spirits, visit our website:
www.spookstospirits.com

Spooks to Spirits Travel Guide
Let local businesses serve all your needs!

Spas
Desirant Day Spa & Salon
Urban Bliss Salon & Spa
Aqua Holistic Skin Care
Spa Cha Cha

Tanning Salons
A Ray Of Sun
Cindy's Body Shop
Bronze Bodies Tanning
The Ultimate Tan & Spa
Sun Shack Tanning and Fitness, LLC

Fun for all Ages
Evergreen Aviation Air & Space Museum - Imax Theater
Ninety-Nine West Twin Cinemas & Drive-In Theatres
Third Street Pizza & Moonlight Theater
Flying M Ranch - Horseback riding
Gallery Theatre - Live Theater
McMinnville Aquatic Center
Chehalem Aquatic Center
Cameo Theatre

Spa cha cha
Luxury spa
Boutique
Massage
Facials
503.883.0220
214 ne evans
downtown

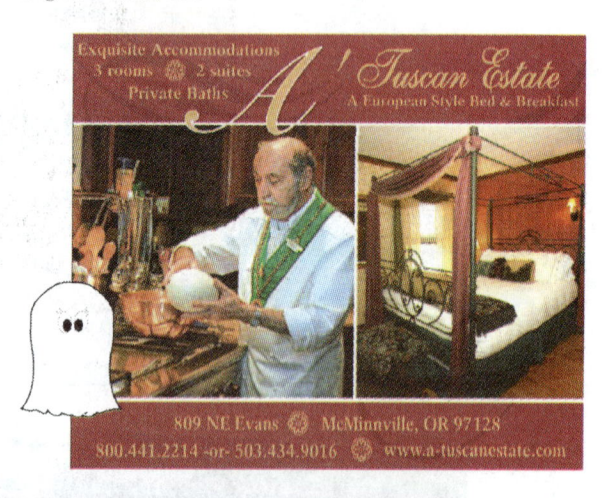

A' Tuscan Estate
A European Style Bed & Breakfast
Exquisite Accommodations
3 rooms — 2 suites
Private Baths
809 NE Evans — McMinnville, OR 97128
800.441.2214 -or- 503.434.9016 — www.a-tuscanestate.com

Kelty Estate
Bed & Breakfast
and
Wedding Center
Lafayette, Oregon
800-867-3740

If you would like to advertise with Spooks To Spirits, visit our website:
www.spookstospirits.com

Spooks to Spirits Travel Guide
Let local businesses serve all your needs!

Beauty Salons & Services
A Ray of Sun
Classic Hair Design
Down 2 Details
French Twist
Hair Care & Co
Rhapsody
Tangles
Tres Beau
Twist Salon
Urbanbliss Salon & Spa
Young's Innovative Hairstyling

Specialty Services
Electrolysis Clinic
Newberg Women's Clinic
Richard Ecker, MD

RV Parks
Olde Stone Village Manufactured Home & RV Park
Wandering Spirit RV Park

DELUXE BILLIARDS
McMinnville, OR 503.472.7571

Union BLOCK Market Place
Our shop is brimming full of Antiques, Furniture, Vintage, Collectibles, Primitives, and Gifts...
...Come and see what's new!
FIND US ON FACEBOOK!
Union Block Marketplace
Antiques & Gifts
Store Hours: Mon - Sat 10-5pm & Sunday 12-4pm • Monthly First Friday Art Walk 5-9pm
616 E. First in Newberg • 503-538-8655
Quality Vendors Welcome - Call or stop by for information.

Joy Hypnotherapy
REMEMBER • HEAL • LOVE
503-910-8873
Got Ghost?

If you would like to advertise with Spooks To Spirits, visit our website:
www.spookstospirits.com

Spooks to Spirits Travel Guide
Let local businesses serve all your needs!

Airplane Services
Aerotron Air Power
NW Air Repair
Sportsman Airpark Ink
Royal Shuttle Airport Services

Limousine, Taxi, Auto Rental
Action Limousine Service
BD Express
Enterprise
Luxury Limo of Oregon
Royal Shuttle Airport Service
Shamrock Taxi

NW Food & Gifts

Gourmet Foods
Wine
Artisan Gifts
Custom Gift Baskets

445 NE 3rd Street
McMinnville, Oregon
(503) 434-6111
www.NWFoodAndGifts.com

Jack of All Beads

Beads & Handcrafted Jewelry

503-474-0611
WWW.JACKOFALLBEADS.COM
618 NE 3RD ST, MCMINNVILLE

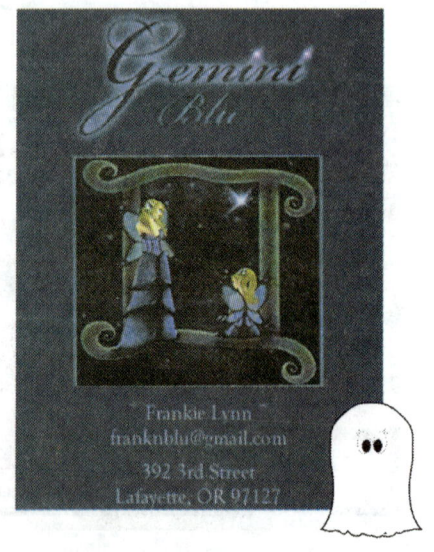

Grandma's Weddings

Wedding Gowns, Bridesmaids Mothers & Flower Girls
Plus Sizes, Alterations and Layaways
Ask About A Mini-Honeymoon

Since 1981
Call For An Appointment
800-670-1735 • 503-472-1735
1030 NE Baker St • McMinnville 97128

Gemini Blu

Frankie Lynn
franknblu@gmail.com
392 3rd Street
Lafayette, OR 97127

If you would like to advertise with Spooks To Spirits, visit our website:
www.spookstospirits.com

Spooks to Spirits Travel Guide
Let local businesses serve all your needs!

Pet & Veterinary Services
Country Kitty Kondo LLC
Pets Stop Inn Boarding & Freeman Retrievers LLC
Tresa Apke DVM
Baker Street Animal Hospital
Barbara J Wynne DVM
Carlton Veterinary Hospital
McMinnville Veterinary Hospital
McMinnville Wildlife Rehabilitation & Care Center
Newberg Veterinary Hospital
Third Street Veterinary Hospital PC
Valley Equine Veterinary Service

Auto
Jiffy Lube
Oil Can Henry's
Texaco Xpress Lube
Xpress Lube

Rental Services
Hertz Equipment Rental Corp
Rent A Center

BARLOW'S PRINTING CO.
Est. 1945

Kyle Eisenbraun

503.472.7711 · 888.472.6086
Fax 503.434.5256

1629 NE Baker St.
PO Box 787
McMinnville, OR
97128

barlowsprintingco@gmail.com

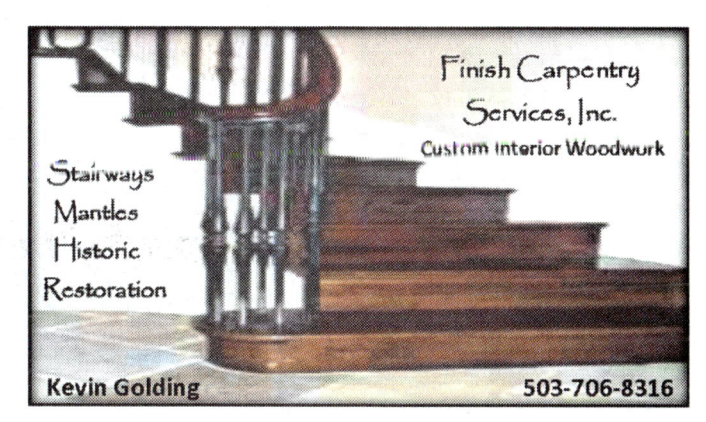

Finish Carpentry Services, Inc.
Custom Interior Woodwork

Stairways
Mantles
Historic
Restoration

Kevin Golding
503-706-8316

If you would like to advertise with Spooks To Spirits, visit our website:
www.spookstospirits.com

References and Credits

Yamhill County Historic Society

Yamhill County Genealogical Society

McMinnville Downtown Historic Registry

McMinnville Downtown Association

Willamette Heritage Center at The Mill

Marion County Historical Society

McMenamins Historic Department

Descendants of the Mercer Family and Abigail Scott Duniway

Descendants of Cornelius Kelty

Owner, LaRambla

Owner, Old Elks Building

Owner, Mack Theater and building

Owner, Roadhouse Pub

Owner, Kelty Estates

"Lafayette Museum" by Bob Thomas

Necktie Parties-Legal Executions in Oregon 1851-1905 by Diane L. Goeres-Gardner

Chinese in the Post-Civil War South: A People Without History by Lucy M. Cohen Louisiana

Guide to the A.R. Burbank Papers 1849-1898, University of Oregon Library, Special Collections & University Archives

Untitled article about Dr. Poling, July 1, 1925. Courtesy of Yamhill County Historic Society

Post about Evangelical Church 50th anniversary, January 6, 1938. Published in *The Weekly Telephone*

"Memoir and Resolution on the Death of Hon. B.P. Boise," Oregon Reports # 49, Morrow 1907 Pulished by Goe. A. Bateson& Co., Inc.

"1850-1890: Glory days" by Jim Lockett

"Start in Steam boating" by James D. Miller

"Amos Cook" by K. B. Cook, Oregon Daily Journal, March 22, 1925

"Peoria Party" in Oregon Magazine

"Oregon or the Grave" by Randol B. Fletcher, http://oregonmag.com/OrHistArticle.htm

"History of the early pioneer" NW Volume 1 Oregon 3 pg 350-367

"Welcome to Hotel Oregon" by Kathrine Huit

"City of McMinnville gets a late start" by Jim Lockett

"Samuel (Uncle Sam) Cozine (1820-1897)" pg.3 by Jim Lockett

"Newby's plans attracted railway, bank" by Jim Lockett

"Page from the past" by Jim Lockett

"First McMinnville Settler Staked Claim In 1844" News Register 1859 reprint 1959

"Yamhill County Courthouse History"

"Historic downtown McMinnville gives glimpse into past" by Patrick Johnson

Yamhill County Circuit Court – Oregon Judicial Dept. website
Perspectives: Yamhill Co 3/6/1989
NowPublic: Crowd Powered Media, www.nowpublic.com

"Underground city found in Pendleton potholes" by Finn J.D. Jonn, http://www.offbeatoregon.com/H1001e_Pendleton.html

"Chinese American History" on Wikipedia

"The Mysterious Underground of Pendleton Oregon" by David Jennings, http://jenningsdavidl.newsvine.com/_news/2008/09/06/1836182-the-mysterious-underground-of-pendleton-oregon

"Historian explore tunnels beneath Salem" by The Associated Press, http://www.oregonlive.com/pacific-northwest-news/index.ssf/2010/10/historians_explore_tunnels_beneath_salem.html

Ghosts of America, www.ghostsofamerica.com

C.A.S.P.E.R. Ghost Hunters, http://caspergh.com/

Oregon Live, www.oregonlive.com

The Linfield Review, http://www.linfield.edu/linfield-review/

Oregon.com

The Boo Crew Credits

Spooks to Spirits
Researched, written and directed by
Tracey Ward

Book Credits

Editing
Caitlin Halvorson

Cover Art Design
Tara Shirriff

Still Photography
Tara Shirriff
Victoria Ward
Eric Rose

Still Shots Courtesy of
Marilyn and Matt Worrix
La Rambla
McMenamins
Panther Creek
Kelty Estate

Still Shot Talent
Victoria Ward- Q6 Talent Portland
Sid Chapman
Nobel Chapman
Cameran Strybing

CD Talent

Narration
Lars Ward

Anna Marple
Jackie Salkield

Reverend Poling
Chanse Orvin

Judge Boise
Glen Van De Veere

Daniel Poling
Noble Chapman

Richard Marple
Michael Miller

Production
Gareth Porter, Grunt Dungeon Studio

Piano
Victoria Ward

Design CD cover
Tara Shirriff

Guitar
Alex Ward

"Season of the Witch"
Donovan

Web Design
Caitlin Halvorson

For more information visit our website at www.spookstospirits.com

CALENDAR OF EVENTS

Monthly wine tasting, Live Theater, and live entertainment are a staple here in Yamhill County. Evergreen Museum and IMAX. Plus Movies with pizza and wine so fun to find and spend some time. Exploring will be the best part of your experience.

JANUARY
McMinnville's Public Market opens for the weekends
3rd Saturday McMinnville Art & Wine Walk
Sunrise Rotary Crab and Oyster Feast

FEBRUARY
McMinnville's Public Marketplace, weekends
Mayor's Charity Ball, McMinnville
Master Gardeners Tree Sale
Native Plant Sale
Euphoria: Wine and Chocolate Weekend

MARCH
The Sip: Wine & Food Classic
Monthly Wine Tasting county-wide
3rd Saturday McMinnville Art & Wine Walk

APRIL
Mac Crab Feed & Auction
Hawaiian Club Luau, Linfield College
Easter Egg Hunts, McMinnville Parks
Easter Bunny Soar-In, Evergreen Air Museum
Easter Special

MAY
Talent and Wine abound!
Mothers Day specials
Cinco de Mayo celebrations
Alien Daze Parade and Celebration, McMinnville
Memorial Day Boat Races, Newberg

JUNE
Brown Bag Concerts downtown Mac, every Thursday noon-1:30
McMinnville's Farmers Market opens Thursdays downtown
Sheridan Days & Pancake Breakfast
Wings & Wheels Fly-In Pancake Breakfast, McMinnville
Carlton Fun Days
McMinnville Summer Garden Tour

JULY
Forth of July Celebration, McMinnville
Brown Bag Concerts downtown Mac, every Thursday noon-1:30
McMinnville's Farmers Market, Thursdays
Turkey Rama Festival, Downtown McMinnville
Willamina's Old-Fashioned Forth of July
Yamhill Derby Days
Amity Pancake Breakfast and Vintage Car Show
International Pinot Noir Celebration, Linfield
Dayton Old-Timers Celebration

AUGUST
Valley View Air Show
Concert in the Grove, Linfield
Art & Wine Art Walk
Yamhill County Fair and Rodeo
Carlton's Walk in the Park
Lafayette Heritage Days
Antique Airplane Fly-In McMinnville
Route 99W Car Show
Flapjacks & Fiddles Pancake Feed

SEPTEMBER
3rd Saturday McMinnville Art & Wine Walk
Oregon Vintage Festival

OCTOBER
Safe and Sane Halloween, McMinnville
Art Harvest Studio Tours
Oktoberfest Dinner at St. John's
3rd Saturday McMinnville Art & Wine Walk
ATV Parade Amity
Ballston Turkey Dinner

NOVEMBER
Coastal Hills Art Tour
Santa's Parade and Tree-Lighting, McMinnville
Wine Thanksgiving Open House and Sale
Trail Band Concert

DECEMBER
McMinnville Christmas Open House
Holiday Tour of Homes
Elks Charity Ball
Lots of live entertainment everywhere for good cheer!

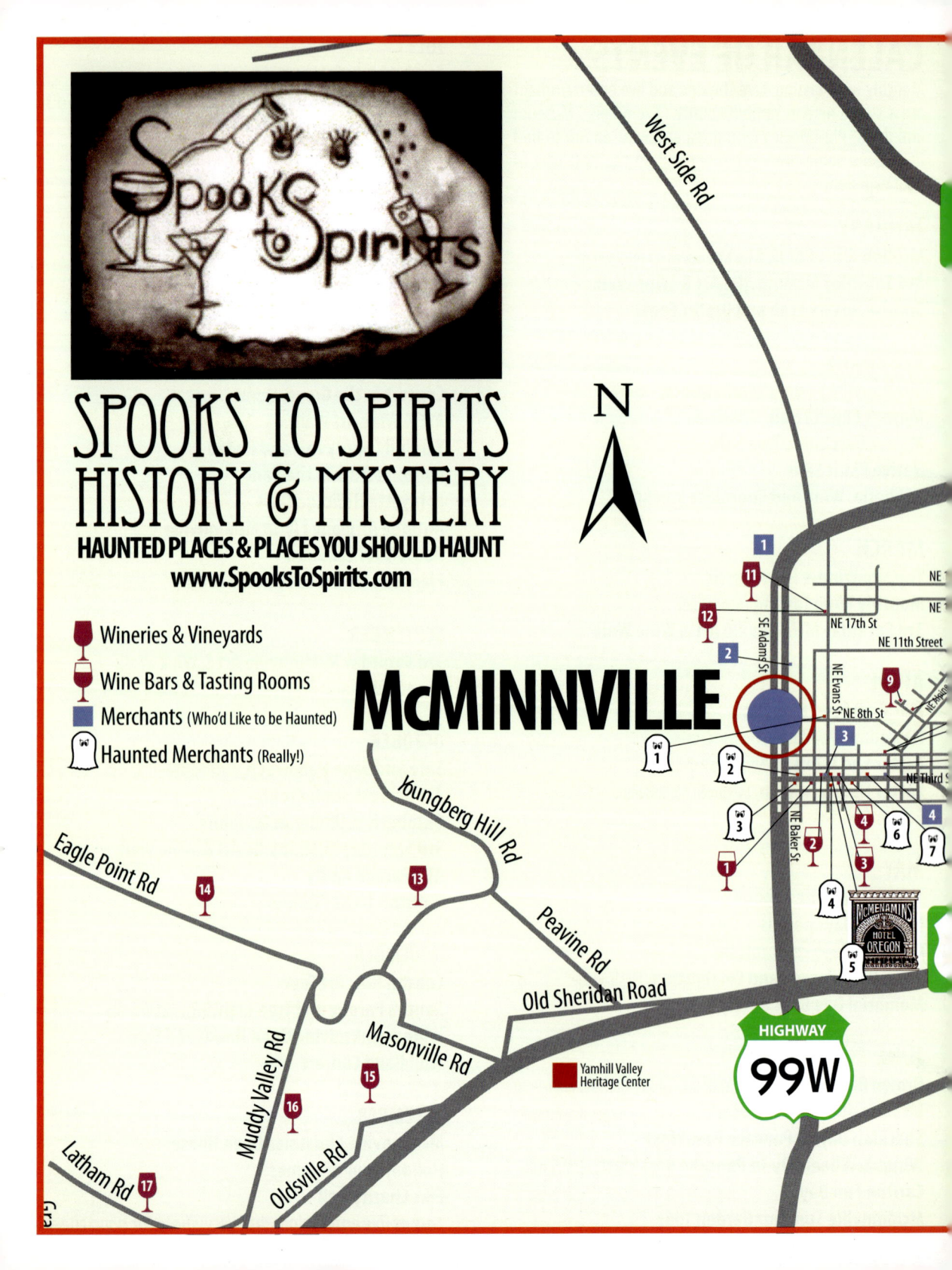

SPOOKS TO SPIRITS
HISTORY & MYSTERY
HAUNTED PLACES & PLACES YOU SHOULD HAUNT
www.SpooksToSpirits.com

- 🍷 Wineries & Vineyards
- 🍷 Wine Bars & Tasting Rooms
- ▪ Merchants (Who'd Like to be Haunted)
- 👻 Haunted Merchants (Really!)

McMINNVILLE

HIGHWAY 99W

47
Mineral Springs Road
Abbey Road
Yamhill County Historical Society
Stoller Road
Archery Summit Rd
Brayman Orchards Rd
Sokol Blosser Lane
McDougall Rd
6th St
Market St
HIGHWAY
99W
18
LAFAYETTE
DA
NE Lafayette Avenue
Street
E First St
NE Three Mile Ln
EVERGREEN
AIR & SPACE MUSEUM
WATER PARK
Comfort INN
H
McMINNVILLE
AIRPORT
233
Amity Dayton Highway
Lafayette Hopewell Highway
Webfoot Road
Wallace Road
Alderman Road
Fairview Road
8

SPOOKS TO SPIRITS
HISTORY & MYSTERY
HAUNTED PLACES & PLACES YOU SHOULD HAUNT
www.SpooksToSpirits.com

WINERIES, VINEYARDS, WINE BARS & TASTING ROOMS

1. Willamette Valley Wine Center
2. NW Wine Company
3. R. Stuart Wine Bar
4. Twelve
5. Panther Creek
6. R. Stuart
7. Anthony Dell Cellars
8. Eyrie
9. Remy
10. Westrey
11. Wineworks Oregon
12. Zivo
13. Youngberg Hill
14. Coeur de Terre
15. Yamhill Valley
16. Maysara
17. Coleman Vineyard
18. Anne Amie
19. Vista Hills
20. Domaine Serene
21. Wine Country Farm
22. Winter Hill
23. White Rose
24. Domaine Drouhin
25. Stoller
26. Durant
27. Sokol Blosser
28. Archery Summit
29. Seufert
30. Hauer of the Dauen

MERCHANTS (Who'd like to be Haunted!)
NP = Not Pictured on Map

1. **Barlow's Printing**
   Commercial Printing, Signs, Banners, Trophies & More
   1629 NE Baker Street; McMinnville, 503-472-7711; barlowsprinting.com

2. **Grandma's Weddings**
   New & Pre-Owned Wedding Gowns, Custom Alterations
   Serving Yamhill County, 503-472-1735; Toll-Free 800-670-1735

3. **Northwest Food & Gifts**
   Gourmet Foods, Wine, Artisan Gifts & Custom Gift Baskets
   445 NE Third Street; McMinnville, 503-434-6111; nwfoodandgifts.com

4. **Golden Valley Brewery**
   Oregon Wines, Full Bar, Full Menu, All Day
   980 E Fourth Street; McMinnville, 503-472-BREW; goldenvalleybrewery.com

5. **Gemini Blu**
   Vintage Clothing & Accessories
   392 Third Street; Lafayette, 971-241-0227

NP **Union Block Marketplace**
Antiques, Furniture, Vintage, Collectibles, Primitives & Gifts
616 E First Street; Newberg, 503-538-8655

NP **Joy Hypnotherapy**
Got Ghosts? Remember, Heal, Love
503-910-8873

NP **Cielo Blu**
Fine Italian Food
119 W Main Street; Carlton, 503-852-6200; cieloblurestaurant.com

NP **Ghost Hill Cellars**
A miner's ghost wanders the hill astride his horse...
12220 NE Bayliss Road; Carlton, 503-852-7347; ghosthillcellars.com

HAUNTED MERCHANTS (Seriously!)

1. **A' Tuscan Estate**
   A European Style Bed & Breakfast; 809 NE Evans Street; McMinnville,
   503-434-9016; Toll-Free 800-441-2214; a-tuscanestate.com

2. **Harvest Fresh Grocery & Deli**
   Natural Produce, Groceries and Delicatessen
   251 NE Third Street; 503-472-5740; harvestfresh.com

3. **La Rambla Restaurant & Bar**
   Northwest Inspired Cuisine from Spain
   238 NE Third Street; McMinnville, 503-435-2126; laramblaonthird.com

4. **Spa Cha Cha**
   Luxury Spa, Boutique, Massage & Facials
   214 NE Evans Street; McMinnville, 503-883-0220

5. **McMenamins Hotel Oregon**
   310 NE Evans Street; McMinnville, 503-472-8427;
   Toll Free 888-472-8427; mcmenamins.com

6. **Jack of All Beads**
   Beads & Handcrafted Jewelry
   618 NE Third Street; McMinnville, 503-474-0611; jackofallbeads.com

7. **Deluxe Billiards**
   Delicious Food, Lottery Games, Beer & Wine, Pool Tables
   711 NE Third Street; McMinnville, 503-472-7571

8. **Kelty Estate**
   Bed & Breakfast and Wedding Center; 675 Third Street; Lafayette,
   503-560-1512; Toll Free 800-867-3740; keltyestate.com

9. **Antonio's Italian Restaurant**
   Delicious Italian Food from Old Family Recipes
   416 E Third Street; Lafayette, 503-864-4182